Verses from Ashes to Ink

Karishma Shingote

Qurate
quratebooks.com

VERSES FROM ASHES TO INK

Karishma Shingote

Published in 2025

© Published by

Qurate
quratebooks.com

Qurate Books Pvt. Ltd.
Goa 403523, India
www.quratebooks.com
Tel: 1800-210-6527, Email: info@quratebooks.com

ISBN: 978-93-58983-85-2

Dedication

The seeds of these poems were often sown in shared moments and solitary reflections. I am deeply grateful to those who have walked alongside me throughout my journey, every person has given me experience, lessons, and learnings. They have sparked and inspired me in many ways. The long walks with myself, the stare in the moonlit lights and thoughts provided the quiet spaces where many of these verses took root.

To those who have shared their journeys, fears, weakness and awakening, thank you for the honest conversations shaping my explorations. Even the tangled threads of darker affections have contributed to this collection's texture. Thank you to everyone who has touched these poems in their becoming, and to you, the reader, for giving them a home.

Preface

These poems emerge from an embrace of complexity, where beauty and struggle coexist. Born in moments of quiet reflection and impassioned expression, they are fragments of a personal journey, echoing experiences of love, loss, and observations of a world simultaneously magnificent and flawed. Within these verses, you will find celebrations of nature's intricate beauty, explorations of love in its diverse forms, a deep yearning for connection, and a conscious rejection of escapism.

They delve into the internal conflicts between thought and feeling, the soul and the human experience. This collection offers a space where the tender vulnerability of longing meets the powerful voice of a desire for change.

Contents

My Being

For my father, the man who was my first home, my guiding light, and my quiet strength. Though you're no longer here, your love still surrounds me in every whisper of the wind, in every star that shines. I miss you every day, but I carry you in my heart—forever and always.

I lost you at an early age.
Still can't turn this drowning page

I learnt to live without you
Difficult to comprehend this truth

My memories of you are very few.
They visit me like a morning dew

I wish I could have you longer.
And see the success I gained

I wish I could see you a little more.
And together our life we could explore

In my joy and happiness I think of you
And in my hard times, praying you'd get me through

I know you are watching me from realm seven.
I know I am taken care of from heaven.

It's been long since I haven't said 'Daddy' aloud.
But in my mind I always hear its sound.

I will always be crowned as "Daddy's Girl"
I am proud to have the best 'Dad' in this world.

Whispers of the Divine

A broken man lost in despair finds hope through divine intervention. No grand miracle, but a soft and guiding touch by grace, he begins to heal, He found his way to healing and a life reborn anew, proving that even the shattered can rise again.

He walked with shadows in his wake, A man once whole, now prone to break.
His eyes held storms, his hands were worn, By battles lost and dreams stillborn.

His spirit fractured, weighted by despair, His a landscape stark and bare
The job was gone, the laughter hushed and still, A hollow echo on a lonely window sill.

Each sunrise brought a heavier, dull ache, A silent question the world refused to take.
The streets he roamed knew his name, But now they watched with silent shame.

No hand reached out, no voice to pierce the gloom, Just the slow settling of his heart's cold tomb.
A thousand prayers, he'd never tried, For God, he swore, had surely died.

But heaven waits in quiet ways, It moves not loud, but through the haze.
And one cold night, with moonlight thin, A spark of something stirred within.

A voice, not loud, not heard with ears, But one that cut through all his fears:
"You're not alone. I've seen you fall, But even broken men can call."

He couldn't name it, couldn't understand, Just a lifting pressure from a weary hand.
He rose unsteadily, his limbs felt strange, Like waking from a sleep that wouldn't change.

He wept, and not from grief this time, But like a sinner touched by rhyme.
He felt a weight begin to rise, Like dawn reborn in tear-stained skies.

Slowly, like a plant towards the sun's embrace, A fragile hope began to find its place.
The weight began to lessen, day by day, As purpose bloomed along his weary way.

He learned to laugh again, a rusty sound, That gradually grew stronger, more profound.
A silent grace, a whisper in the soul, That mended pieces and made him whole.

A Celestial Tie

No matter the time or place, their souls find each other—lovers in one life, strangers in the next, yet always drawn together. Across lifetimes, through fate or chance, their bond refuses to break, whispering of something eternal.

And we met again, as it was destined to be.
And we felt again, as it was meant to be.

Our soul's journey has been written down.
Our Karmas always make us come around

In our conscience, we are always in love with each other.
But down here, we clearly struggle to comprehend one another.

And we met again, as it was destined to be.
And we felt again, as it was meant to be.

Two souls connected through various lifetimes
We had to unite, as our energies are inclined

This divine emotion we always feel makes us reunited.
Our time on earth made our hearts again, ignited

And we met again, as it was destined to be.
And we felt again, as it was meant to be.

Awaiting that in some life, we will be at peace
Hoping that our sail will be like a pleasant breeze.

Our voyage somewhere settles in dwelling together.
Inviting another soul to complete our ménage forever

And we met again, as it was destined to be.
And we felt again, as it was meant to be.

A Dance in Paradise

She stepped into nature and felt an unspoken connection, as if the earth itself recognized her. In its whispers and rustling leaves, she found a sense of belonging that spoke louder than words.

Among the lush greens, it swooped completely by the breeze.
It seemed my body had freezed,
With this unimaginable sacred energy, the soul had seized.

A quiet hush of the sun's setting light. My eyes gazed, the warmth in sight.
Nature signed me to feel free to find myself and dare to dream.

The winds sang and made the trees dance. Tears rolled down my face, like a stream.
Making me feel awakened and whole. In this wanderlust, I found my home

In this realm, I found my grace. A heartfelt connection in this sacred place
As I breathed the fragrance of the air, I felt lighter and all my worries lay bare.

Surrounded by this enchanting nature, like an unearthly joy that I had savored
Felt like I was embraced by the creator, and all the heavens were in my favor.

Just beneath the clear blue skies, my form had wholly arised
So enthralled by this beautiful surprise, I just knew I was in Paradise.

A Heart's Betrayal

He loved her like she was his world, but she shattered it with a kiss that wasn't his. She lost herself in regret, realizing too late that her mistake cost her the only love that felt like home. Now, both stood in the wreckage—broken, but in different ways.

She stood in the doorway, awaiting her final goodbye.
While he sat on the sofa, still assuming why?

There he was, wrapped in silent despair.
Not seeking revenge, but thinking 'is this even fair?'
In pain, he looked up, pondering why the sky was so high.
Wondering what more secrets it's trying to pry

A numbness in his form, still as the night
Yet within his mind, there was a chaotic fight.
Storms of memories clash and collide
While his heart remained hollow inside
Echoes of why, when and how?
The present feels so distant, only the past is now.

He gave her his heart, his trust, his soul.
Yet she played him in a fleeting role.
He speculated when love turned so cruel, and why dreams die.
As tears that he swallowed were burning inside.

He looks up to the high sky, seeking a reply.
But the stars remain silent, cold and dry.
How does love twist into a knife?
Why does betrayal cut through life?
These answers evade him, and he pleads
He is only left to wonder, as his heart aches and bleeds.

She stood in the doorway, awaiting her final goodbye.
With a shattered heart and a regret in her eyes
As she walked down the stairs, heading on to empty terrain
Her mind cluttered from all the mistakes she refrained
All the encounters she had were just for an adrenaline need.
All the meaningless charm, she paid no heed.
It was nothing but a careless spark, a fleeting thrill in the dark.

Love is now broken. A loss of trust puts a scar on the soul.
Even time alone, will not make it whole.
As she wept beneath the moonlit light, fathoming his loss, there
were no new stories to rewrite.

An end to this love and togetherness story
She accepts the journey to be now hard and thorny.

The echoes of their love and laughter were only a past
A silent scream, heavy wounds ...how long will this all last?
No shield could guard their hearts, no walls could defend
A betrayal, a loss that stings with a faithless end.

The Girl She Left Behind

She sometimes yearns for her untamed past, a life filled with danger, passion, and freedom. As she sits in the stillness of her present, she aches for the fire and chaos that once made her feel alive.

There she sits beneath the velvet sky,
Stars flickering like fragments of time gone by.
A quiet ache settles in her chest,
Memories rising, refusing to rest.

She thinks of the woman she used to be,
Wild-eyed, reckless, running free.
Drunk on danger, high on the thrill,
Chasing chaos, bending will.

She wore her sins like second skin,
Found beauty in breaking, joy in the sin.
She craved the fire, danced in pain,

Felt alive in every loss, every gain.
The mess, the madness, how she adored it.
The ache, the chase, she lived for it.
No rules. No peace. Just burning light,
Falling in love with the endless night.

But now she sits in gentler days,
In softened tones and calmer ways.
She wonders when the fire dimmed,
When quiet replaced the life once brimmed.

There's grace in stillness, yes! it's true,
But her soul still echoes a wilder hue.
So here she is, beneath the stars,
Longing for those distant scars.

Not for the pain, not for the cost,
But for the part of her she's lost.
A life unchained, untamed, surpassed,
She yearns to breathe that misty past.

Of Earth and Ether

As she embarks on a mystical journey into the unknown, guided by just an inner calling. She experiences divine and solace through nature—enchanted forests, moonlit paths, and whispering winds—she is slowly awakened to her true self.

She stepped into the veil of the unknown, not lost, but summoned, by whispers of her own.
The woods opened like a memory long buried, branches bending, secrets she carried.
She walked where moonlight kissed the leaves, where silence spoke, and time seemed unweaved.
Each step like a spell, each breath like a hymn, the wild crowned her from root to limb.
The air was thick with sacred things, with unseen hands and muttering wings.
She drank from streams of cold flow, her spirit opened like never before.
The stars bowed low to speak her truth, and winds recalled the song of youth.

The earth enfolded her with grace, no mask, no fear, no need to chase.
Her soul, once caged, now took to flight, cloaked in shadows, bathed in light.
The chaos stilled, the noise grew dim, she met her Self beyond the rim.
Now she walks with peace as kin, her war within turned soft, turned thin.
And in her stillness, she became, both flesh and flame, both wild and tame.

A Kiss that Burned the Soul

Two souls, once intertwined by the past, crossed paths again after years apart. For her, the kiss was electric—deadly, even—pulling buried memories and lost love to the surface. But as she searched his eyes for the same fire, she found only indifference, as if their past had faded to nothing in his mind.

The evening was bright, the place was lit up with ember lights.
They met after years, but still a spark they yearned.

That night was blissful, jazz music playing soulful.
A silence that spoke, underneath a burning desire evoke

A stare a glance, with the mild touch of their hands
Her heart fluttered like wings, her brain felt a tingling.

A sudden kiss sparked a flame, melting all her maim
It was fierce and wild, the feeling undefined.

A deadly kiss, burned the night skies, awoke a storm, held inside
The burning fire, a stolen taste of her deepest desire

All that was regressed came on to the surface.
All her feelings, all her love, came back to the shore.

But nights grew cold when he was gone,
Her heart rewound that kiss till dawn.

The devourer of the kiss, the taste of him, liked salted rain.
Leaving her ghosts that danced inside her veins

Days went by, months were gone. Like whispers fading with the dawn.
But this kiss haunts, a thunder's cry, still lives beneath her every sigh.

No time, nor fate could ever dim, the kiss she felt on her every limb.
For once the soul has burned like this, it never heals, it never quits.

Yet every time the shadows fall. She feels the kiss, she hears the call.
She needs him, like the night fancies the skies with unshed tears behind her eyes.

An After Life Promise

A poignant story of two souls bound by an unspoken yet profound love, enduring even through death. As she holds onto hope after his passing, their love ultimately reunites them beyond this life—in a place where time no longer matters.

I saw them. I felt them.
Their love, wordless, yet resounding. Their bond was unbreakable, even as time slipped away.
They were madly in love, concerned yet composed,
Knowing this was their final act, and still, they stood strong.

I saw them. I felt them.
The way she spoke in glances, the way he answered with a smile.
Her laughter lit up the air; his eyes, soft with knowing.
They didn't just love—they understood.
Completely. Silently. Truly.

I saw them. I felt them.
He was fading. She was aching.
Still, she wrapped him in strength, in hope, in presence.
He knew: without words, she was there,
And she had never let go. This… this was love.

I saw them. I felt them.
He lay still, breathing his last, eyes tracing the memories of their past.
A final smile, a whispered vow:
“I’ll be with you always—our love will outlast us even now.”

I saw her. And I felt her.
The silence. The space he left behind.
The aching hope of seeing him once more,

To feel his warmth, his breath, his soul.
She lived on—for that hope, for that promise,
That they would meet again, beyond time.

And one gentle day,
She climbed the golden steps,
Met by the eyes she had never forgotten.

Their love—eternal—reunited in the stars.
Not a dream, not a wish.
But forever, at last.

Thorns Beneath Her Skin

The inner torment of a woman trapped in emotional damage and denial, whose unresolved pain poisons her relationship and identity. Unable to face her truth, she clings to blame and illusion, ultimately becoming consumed by her own wounds.

She was deeply wounded, in the marrow of her spirit,
where secrets hide and sorrow seeds.

She wore her damage like an heirloom, kept close, clenched in trembling hands.
Blame became her compass, he was the storm she could withstand.

Toxic, the air around her grew, like thorns in gardens left untrimmed.
She twisted truths into a noose, and wrapped it round both her and him.

She could not leave, nor let him go, addicted to the ache they shared.
Two hearts in torment, bonded only by the fear she never dared.

She was deeply wounded, a prisoner of her past designs,
entangled in her own misdeeds, lost between the fault lines.
She lashed like serpents coiled tight, around his soul, she did constrict.
Escaping truth, embracing lies, her world split—dark and contradict.

She could not yield, nor own her wrongs, a mirror cracked, yet never turned.
And so she danced with shadows, in a fire she'd long since burned.

She was deeply wounded, adrift in thought, in silent screams,
trapped beneath a glassy surface, sinking in her fractured dreams.

Alone, she sat with open wounds, unhealed by time, unbent by grace.
Love a ghost she couldn't hold, narcissism carved upon her face.

A Maze of Mind

Overthinking creates a loop of endless doubts and assumptions, making your mind believe even the most unrealistic fears are true. It distorts reality, turning possibilities into certainties, even when there's no real evidence.

Overthinking is such an uncanny thing.
It makes your brain sting.

You make up your own stories and imagine the worst
Until your heart shatters and bursts

It makes you feel dejected, and you feel it's realistic.
Making you feel dispirited and going all ballistic

It's like a demon dominating you.
It's like an evil spirit possessing you.

You want to get out, but your brain loves to feed on it.
It's like a drug. You are addicted to it.

Even though you are not living the stories, you begin to
experience them.
Even though it's draining you, undermining you, you find solace
in them.

How your mind can be your own enemy, making you live in this
illusion
Fabricating unknown tales from a figment of your imagination.

A Warrior Within

A young artist's journey navigating bipolar disorder is depicted through his use of color and painting as coping mechanisms, ultimately spreading positivity through his art.

A man of a thousand faces, and muddled thoughts, who would always change his skin
A man reflecting different moods, a different life, that's how society described him

But he was an artist at heart, exploring different colors and capturing different essences
Though beneath the surface of a creative genius, he struggled with a silent obsolescence

Days of rollercoaster of emotions, some mornings feeling invincible, where the mind races with notions
Some days, without any warning, darkness would descend, and his thoughts go, in explosions

Some days, his brushstrokes, bold and confident, and his art flourished
Some days, colors would fade, and the world would become dull, and hopes tarnished

Despite the turmoil and unpredictability haze of these sensations
Somewhere deep inside, his art made him feel compassion

A gentle touch, his tender hands, In art's embrace, he makes his stand
Though commotion reigns, and sometimes doubts ignite, the strokes of colors transcend

He learnt the signs of his inconsistent feelings, and navigated the uncertain landscape
Finding ways to manage the trait and celebrate the minds of clarity, allowing it to reshape

He painted tales of his inner strife, His art a mirror to his life journey
No more, silent battles rage within, but a testament to the strength of the human spirit.

He showed the world that even in the grip of ailment, the soul can burn brighter
An unshaken strength and unwavering belief, suffering becomes a battle cry, not a surrender

A Wandering Solitude

Longing for an escape and the chance to rediscover herself, she decides to embark on an uncharted journey in search of solitude and renewal. Her travels lead her to breathtaking landscapes and quiet moments of reflection, where she begins to confront her innermost fears and desires, A solo trip, a heartwarming tale of awakening the person inside of you to embrace the journey and savor life's nuances, for they hold more meaning than the destination.

She was weighed down by heartbreak and trapped in the
monotony of an unfulfilling existence.
She longed for an escape and a chance to rediscover herself to
embark on an uncharted journey.

A place where she would find solace and renewal
A place where she could find her vanished spirit

A road trip far off, from her past and dreary life
She ventured into unknown terrain, with fear and excitement in
her eyes.

A beauty in nature, the calmness in the waters is what she sought after.
She let herself be completely mesmerised by the scenic views of a different consciousness.

Her face glowed, and her heart felt the warmth of the season.
She could hear the ocean's breath and feel the cool breeze whisper in her form.

Lush green trees and colourful flowers made her life blissful and empowering.
The waves kissed her feet, her body went into shivers.

Breathtaking tapestry of life, woven with the colours of earth, sky, and water
Birds sing melodies of freedom and rivers carve paths with patient grace.

The journey leads her to beautiful landscapes and quiet moments.
To reflect and confront her innermost fears and desires

A path she felt awakened, the love she never nurtured.
The flow of her essence to the core, she bore

This wandering solitude made a heartwarming tale.
In nature's womb, she found peace and a reminder that all is beautifully
Interconnected.

To accept the facts and understand -
"The road itself is where we grow - not just the place we long to go"

And....We got Strayed!

She gave her heart away, only to be left with empty promises and fading memories. Love once bloomed in her soul, but he walked away, leaving nothing but echoes of what could have been. In the end, she learned that some loves are meant to be lost.

Your presence in my life had a lovely essence.
Your abandoning me was a dreadful vision.

When you kissed me for the first time, you blew me off my feet.
When you hurt me for the first time, my heart could not bear this deceit.

Your touch made my senses go high.
And deep down, I knew this was just a lie.

You made me experience the love I never knew.
You also made my heart ache that I could never get through.

Your domineering behaviour compelled me to succumb to you.
Your deceiving character made me feel blue.

You knew I loved you and were aware of my fears.
You witnessed my pain, and saw my heart being speared
But you never felt the need to mend these tears.

Falling in love with you was my choice.
But falling out of love was fate's choice.

We now only have some bittersweet memories.
We live with each other only in our own fantasies.

Dance...to Unheard Tunes

The emotional struggle of a man who yearns for deep connection but hesitates to fully embrace his feelings, an emotional tension of someone yearning to feel, to accept vulnerability, but struggling to surrender and accept what you feel completely, it's a plea for vulnerability, intimacy, and emotional honesty.

This ink you bleed, it wants to speak.
A buried truth, a secret ache so deep.

What is it that keeps you yearning,
A fire in you, always burning?

What do you chase in shadows and sleep,
A longing so loud, yet silence you keep?

Don't silence these rising vibrations,
Don't fear this pull, this sweet persuasion.

Feel it, don't fold beneath the weight.
Let emotion in. It isn't too late.

No shame in wanting. No sin in need.
No fault in softness, no guilt to feed.

Let me in, beyond the guarded glance,
I see your ache, I crave this dance.

The warmth you crave, I hold the flame.
Our hearts could beat in the same name.

So move to this rhythm you barely hear,
Breathe in the truth you've kept unclear.

Your eyes, they beg for connection,
But your heart delays confession.

Still, I am here, open and known
Loving even the pieces you've never shown.

A Tapestry of Strength

A woman's strength is not just in her resilience, but in her ability to nurture and inspire. She stands as a pillar of courage, weathering life's storms with grace and determination. Her heart is a fortress of hope, guiding others through the darkest of times.

A story of a young and beautiful maiden
A tale of her strength and life that remains unshaken

A child like essence, pure and bright, with innocence that shines like light.
Her heart, so full of love and grace, can lift you to a higher place.

In her shadows deep, lie too many sorrows
She lost a close, an undescribed feeling of pain below

Her heart was left in the depths of woe
But in her spirit of hope and love, light still glowed

Life planted many downfalls and lessons to learn
She kept the braveness and never let the flame burn

A mind alive with endless possibilities, a soul that shines like a beacon in the night
She faces challenges and loss, though she remains steadfast and fights

Her journey is a tale of trials and triumphs, of moments that define her grace and beauty.
She is a figure of elegance; a warrior of the heart, armed with the power of resilience and the wisdom of duty

A lesson, a reminder to many that even in the darkest of times, there is always a light that guides us forward.
Inspiring all to stand courageously and endure power in the face of adversity and look onward

Stone Heart, Soft Words

Their hearts were charmed by each other's smiles, unaware of the "horror stories" being compiled. She believed he was her protector who rescued her from past struggles, only to realize he was to become captor, guilty of a profound betrayal. Now she feels caged in his arms. A disillusionment and anguish of discovering that love has transformed into a form of imprisonment.

"Release me now, I beg, I plead!" This unseen snare, how tightly it's decreed.
Our love, I thought, a boundless flight, Unknowing then, each gesture veiled the blight.
Each smile you cast, my senses would betray, Concealing tales that steal my light away.
I believed our love, a freedom taking hold, But every act, a story left untold
My foolish heart, it fluttered at your grace, While you were weaving horrors in this place.

"Unwind this hold, I cry, I strain!" This phantom coil binds me in its reign.

My heart would leap whenever you drew near, Oblivious to the darkness drawing clear.

I saw a shield, a haven strong and true, But found instead, a hand that would undo.

"Let me go! I'm suffocating here!" This invisible chain tightens all my fear.

You promised solace from the inner fight, Not knowing then, you'd plunge me into night.

I sought a savior, steadfast and so brave, Unknowing then, the one who would enslave.

I dreamt our love, a spirit untamed, But every touch, a cruel deception framed.

A guardian's guise, I blindly did embrace, Not seeing then, the ruin in your trace.

"Release me now, I beg, I plead!" This unseen snare, how tightly it's decreed.

A Poor Little Rich Girl

She was born into wealth but felt trapped in a golden cage. Her heart longed for colors and canvases, yet duty bound her to boardrooms and family legacies. Every stroke she painted in secret felt like rebellion, but the weight of heritage kept her brushes locked away. Torn between passion and responsibility, she watched her dreams fade like an unfinished masterpiece, knowing the price of privilege was her own freedom.

She was born with a silver spoon
But... never thought of it as a boon.

She had everything, but still nothing

She swam in all the luxuries of life.
But she did not feel the essence of self-drive.

She had an eye for creativity.
But... never considered it as a priority.

She was to look after the generational heritage.
And maintain this high vintage

Her dreams were just dreams.
Her passion became her regression

Felt lonely in this chaotic crowd
She desired to make herself feel proud.

But she had no courage to step out.
As her mind was drowning in doubts

Dressed up in richness, draped in pearls
She was just a poor little rich girl.

Tethered to Yesterday

Despite the passage of time and attempts to connect with others, the lingering memories and emotional attachment to a former lover continue to haunt him. He feels guilt, emotional paralysis, and a deep sense of being spiritually and mentally bound to the past, making it nearly impossible to start anew or let anyone else in.

It's so hard to move on,
So hard to let it go.
Though months have passed since they split apart,
A fresh beginning feels hollow, slow.

Each time he gets close to someone new,
Her shadow lingers, breaking through.
His lips may touch another's skin,
But memories of her flood back in.

His mind, a maze of guilt and regret,
Haunted by love he can't forget.
No one gets close, no one gets in—
He believes his longing is a kind of sin.

He's anchored deep in yesterday,
Drifting farther from today.
Caught in echoes, trapped in then,
He wonders if he'll feel whole again.

It's so hard to move on,
So hard to let her go.
He's still chained to what has been,
Unable to let the past outflow.

Becoming!!

Life tested her with hardships, failures, and fleeting chances, yet she embraced them all. Each step, whether painful or uncertain, shaped her into something stronger. This was not just survival—it was her becoming.

She was given a unique opportunity to rise to the best version of herself,
She embarked on a path of discovering who she is meant to be for herself.

She was put in deep water. She was asked to face the storms.
She was sent hardships and failures in her life, which put her in swarms.

The paths that lay ahead of her came with a great cost.
Where she needed to sacrifice, promises and dreams needed to be lost

To cross the threshold of a new journey,
She had to let go and break the past key.

She had to show up in the world and face the squall,
Embrace the truth, the new beginnings to end this brawl.

She came to a place of acceptance, taking her deeper,
And she watched the old drift into the ether.

Then the chapter of her life suddenly changed, and the story was rewritten.
Life then came around, and she felt whole, and the sun had risen.

Everything cleared, and a beautiful divine path she could see.
And she became what she was meant to be.

In Someone Else's Fire

The intensity, conflict, and emotional surrender tied to infidelity. She experienced the exciting and unfamiliar thrill of another one, finding her intensely drawn to someone other than her partner. A secret encounter, feeling a strong sense of being wanted and a lack of guilt or remorse in the moment.

The night was a different high— A thrill so fierce, she couldn't deny.

A scent of shadowed, forbidden delight,
A touch that burned in the cloak of night.
Hunger whispered through every pore,
Lust like waves—she begged for more.

Fingers danced on her naked soul,
His kisses wild, his body bold.
His tongue—a fire that knew no shame,
Drew surrenders from her lips, her name.

The night was a different high— A thrill so fierce, she couldn't deny.

A quake of pleasure shook her frame,
So raw, so wrong—but none to blame.
Euphoria cloaked in mystery's veil,
Too rapt, too far gone, to bail.

Desire screamed where reason died,
She chased the ache she couldn't hide.
A passion fierce, uncaged, unkind—
No rules, no lines, just flesh and mind.

The night was a different high— A thrill so fierce, she couldn't deny.

He waited at home—her partner, her vow,
The one she once needed, not needed now.
But here she lay in another's arms,
Drenched in heat, undone by charm.

These lurid thoughts, they made her bold,
The thought of being desired—bought and sold.
No guilt, no second glance behind—
Just hunger fed and freedom blind.

No guilt. No shame.
Just heat. Just flame.
A need too sharp to pacify,
A thirst she fed beneath a lie.

The night was a different high— A thrill so fierce, she couldn't deny.

And she found.... Eternal Peace!!

She fought endlessly—for love that slipped away, for money that never lasted, for a family that never stood by her. No matter how hard she tried, life always found a way to break her. In death, she finally found the peace that eluded her in life.

Time and time again, she went through the same pattern.
A heartbreak, a betrayal, her trust was always broken.

She questioned, Why would this be happening?
What is the reason for all this repeating?

She searched, prayed, and begged for answers.
Trying to understand why life puts her through disasters

Always hoping for a Ray of light,
She would always stay strong and put up a fight.

But, how long could she put up a brave face?
Her life was shattered, nothing to hold and no one to embrace.

Down under, she was exhausted and broken.
Feeling lonely, cold, famished, and frozen

Tired and weary of the emotional tussle
Her mind and body gave in to this hustle.

In this battle between her brain, life, and heart
She kept on reliving her past.
And one fine day, she gave in and breathed her last

End to all her sufferings
Unanswered questions quietly burying
She lay on the earth.... Ah! Las!! Peacefully sleeping

The Weight She Wore

She is haunted by a dark past filled with regret and self-inflicted emotional wounds. She reflects on the pain she caused and the mistakes she made now remains trapped in her own guilt. She now doesn't seek forgiveness from him but longs for inner peace—a release from the crushing weight of who she once was.

She walked alone beneath a starless sky,
The night had stretched endless, it was silent, cold, and wide.
Each step echoed louder than the last, like the darkness
whispered of her past.

Long ago, she planted seeds in poisoned soil
Some choices made in haste, many words laced with deceit,
A love she tortured, a heart turned cruel.
She knew now or probably, she had known for some time.

The wind pressed against her like judgment, shivering her bones,
shaking loose the fragments of a version of herself she no
longer wished to be.
The stars, once which were her comfort, now felt like piercing
eyes watching, condemning, and judging her trials,
Reflecting the fire, She had once lit in others' lives, fire that
burned
too wild to contain.

Her mind was crowded, riddled with questions, she already knew
the answers to.
Why did she do it? How could she? Could she ever be forgiven?
She fought shadows that didn't belong to anyone else, but only
hers, and they clung to her heels, dragging her down into herself.

The moonlight, fractured through clouds, highlighted the parts
of her,
she wished she could erase moments of weakness, manipulation,
betrayal.
No one judged her now, because no one knew.
But she judged herself. In this guilt trip she laid

She had seen the truth behind her own mask, the hurt she caused,
the silence she weaponized.
And though she had changed, though she had let go of the
wrong,
the wrong had not let go of her.

Each prayer she whispered, wasn't for redemption, it was for
peace.
A quiet mercy to hush the storm within.
She didn't want to be saved.
She only wanted to stop drowning in the weight of the woman
she used to be.

Awakening the Light Within!!

In the quiet of her breath, she sank deep — Beyond the noise, beyond the ache, She rose from the silence, not empty, but armed — Ready for another war, because she finally knew, Everything she needed was already within.

A sudden cold rushed into her form. All the old began to deform
She felt this overcharged sorrow, unaware why the feeling made her feel so hollow.
Tears rolled down her cheek, but a sigh of relief was heaved.

This overwhelming feeling, she's trying to gather its meaning.
She closed her eyes to escape the noise, but found her universe behind her lids.
Each breath peeled away the weight she carried, until silence wrapped her like a warm light.

Watery-eyed, she gained some answers.
Stood there her Angel, to grant her a boon she was eager to bear.
The meditation awakened the hidden energies, which were being suppressed mentally.

Gathering her emotions, thinking about the Her Angels comment, she wanted to know what it actually meant.
Whispered a voice within her…which said
"All the repressed emotions have resurfaced to the core.
Indicating to make you stronger and powerful to fight a new war".
That peace was never outside. It was always her own.

Echoes of You

She aches for his presence, haunted by memories of laughter and love that now feel like a distant dream. Every moment without him is a silent punishment, a reminder of the pain she caused. In losing him, she finally understands what he truly meant.

This longingness is driving me insane.
Each thought of you is endless and in vain.
Waiting for you is a consuming pain.
This yearning for you a bittersweet refrain

I see you in my dreams, a divine vision.
Where my imagination takes me to the bright skies
A feeling of togetherness where my being delights

I see you in my tears, with joyful eyes.
I hear your voice whispering about our heavenly ties.
Hoping one day our love will arise

My embodiment wants to feel your touch, my heart to sense the embrace.
Through time and space, your presence stays like a haunting melody in life's endless maze.

My heart is a prisoner, bound in chains, hence waiting for you is driving me insane.
I know this pain is my penitence, which I shall bear in silence.
Hoping one day I will be forgiven for my damnation

Art of Letting Go

Release the weight of what once was, no longer clinging to ghosts of the past. Some things are meant to fade, making space for what's yet to arrive. Letting go wasn't losing—it was trusting that life had more to offer. With an open heart, step forward, ready for the beauty of what comes next.

Every story comes with an ending, things left unanswered, the moments unresolved.
Every goodbye teaches us something, a breakthrough and a being to be evolved.

In this empty space we need some closure.
In this silence, there comes some composure.

We seek healing not in the answers, but in the strength we discover within.
We strip away from our illusions of control and rise to win.

The danger of expectations comes from holding onto a possibility
Then we face uncertainty, but in the same place we find tranquillity.

We condemn ourselves and hold on to the shadows of the past.
We confront our pain, forgive ourselves and now solace has surpassed

Steeped in ambiguity leaves a haze of chaos and the absence of the truth becomes an ache.
Yet within this discomfort lies an invitation not to grieve but to grow and heaviness to break.

Life rarely gives us a resolution we crave. Our hearts need a conclusion to move ahead.
But life is not meant to be understood at every moment. Not every story comes to a happy end.

The art of letting go is acceptance and embracing the bonds of loss, with no bitter pain.
A soul to release for that Love once held it's time to set it free and hearts to unchain

Heartfelt Resonance

From the moment their eyes met, the world around them faded into silence, as if time itself had paused to witness their union. Their souls recognize each other instantly, an unspoken bond weaving between them like a melody only they could hear. Conversations flowed effortlessly, laughter felt like home. In that one meeting, they knew—they had found the missing piece of their souls.

With wind in her hair and thoughts in her mind, she was sitting by the sea all alone.
A book in her hand, penning down her musings, engaged in its meditation.

As she peered beyond the horizon, she saw an image so pleasing.
It became closer the longer she stared, until he stood across her.

A well-groomed man with a brawny frame, tanned skin, and a smile so charming
A mein so ruggedly tousled, she was totally captured by his essence.

He gazed at her with those expressive eyes, which conveyed
emotion and charisma.
She could not take her eyes off him, and her phiz made it
apparent of her mystical feelings.

They both glanced at each other, and an inexplicable feeling
wavered through their forms.
Generating a cosmic alteration in the environment that
surrounded their allure.

He was seated next to her, with a grin so delightful and a
soothing aura.
Her eyes twinkled with this gesture, and her heart displayed an
Aurora.

An attraction so profound, the words simply had to emerge.
The conversation unfurled their wings, and in each other they
were now completely submerged.

Where two souls met in a tender light; and their love story of
forever began.
As fate wove their paths, it was their karma to be one.

Their hearts were entwined, and they made a solemn vow.
A love to win, through every moment, then and now.

Across the ages and through the years, a melody that makes them
whole
These souls resonated, and forever, their love continues to grow.

When the Darkness Wore a Smile

A beautiful soul falls for a mysterious woman who takes advantage of his vulnerability. Betrayed and broken, he loses faith in love and retreats into solitude, choosing silence over connection.

He was handsome, pleasing and a loving soul, and behind his charming eyes was a man ablaze with sorrow.
His past clung on to him like smoke: abandonment, rejection, he never cradled in lovers arms,
But still searching for a place to call home.
He wandered through crowds, but felt unseen,
longing for something more than passing smiles, for warmth that stayed,
And wished for a love that didn't leave.

Then she came. A woman cloaked in mystery, dressed in black, eyes like nightfall.
She didn't knock, she just entered, and he let her in,
Her smile for him was like a dancing melody, her touch for him was adrenaline heavenly

They fell for each other, deep and intense.
To him, she was a muse, a rhythm to his unexplored heart.
To her, he was sweetness to be devoured, and a vulnerability to be used.

He loved recklessly, open-heartedly, believing in the softness of her words.
But she: she wove illusions with lips like fire, feeding on his tenderness, drinking from the well of his trust.
She never loved him. She needed control. She wanted him to be under her wings

Bit by bit, she unraveled him, not with rage, but with indifference.
She clipped the wings of his spirit and toyed with the strings of his heart,
until all that remained was a man confused by cruelty in the shape of intimacy.

He asked himself, again and again,
Why would someone kiss what they planned to break?
Why offer warmth only to steal the flame?

And so, he folded into himself. Broken and distant.
Alive, but dulled.
He stopped believing in love, shut the door to his heart,
and chose silence over connection.

Now he craves nothing, no companion, no belonging, no whispered dreams in the dark.
Only solitude. Only sleep.
Only distance from the shadow of what once felt like love.

A Divine Ray of Light

Their souls recognize each other long before their eyes ever met, bound by something ancient and unbreakable. In every glance, every touch, there was a knowing—an unspoken language only they could understand, echoing across lifetimes.

A Divine harmony of two souls meeting,
That's how she resonates with this angelic partnering.

He reads through her eyes, he feels through her Aura,
He makes her feel alive and awakens her spirit to an enchanting plethora.

His words for her are a beautiful melody.
His loving and caring embrace just makes her feel pretty.

His gentle touch creates a sparkle in her charm.
Transforming her dark side into a chiseled, loving form

He lifts her soul with a tender grace.
In his gaze she finds a sacred place.

Through his caress, her doubts disperse.
She now rewrites her heart's purpose

He is a guiding light to her lost world, on to a steady stream.
He gives her – her own life filled with the truest dreams.

A Winter's Dream

They share meaningful conversation, dance to the rhythm of their bond, and eventually become physically and emotionally intimate. In his presence, she feels alive and cherished, as if she's blooming with joy. Though she awakens to reality, the feeling of love and wonder lingers, leaving her inspired and hopeful as a daydreamer holding onto the beauty of that imagined moment.

On a cold winter night, she saw him, draped in white, glowing beneath the moon's soft light.
He walked into her world,calm and sure, with a smile that warmed the frost, and a presence that spoke in poetry without words.

There was something different in the way he moved, a style unspoken, a vibe so majestic, like magic written in flesh and soul.

His words carried wisdom, his thoughts spun like stories she'd never heard, novel in every sense, a man made of metaphors and quiet strength.

They spoke like old friends who had only just met. Laughter echoed in between pauses, and between silences, something tender grew.

They danced! not to music they knew, but to the rhythm of shared truths and untold tales. Their stories unfolded like leaves in spring, vulnerable, but alive.

In the hush of the night, they melted into each other, cozy embraces, passionate touches, breath and heartbeats in sync. Love, unspoken yet fully known, was made beneath a fragile moon.

She bloomed in his arms, grateful in the moment, marveling at how something could feel so right without needing to last forever.

But morning came. The warmth faded. He was gone. a dream that dissolved with the rising sun.

Still, his glow lingered. And though the bed was cold, her soul stayed lit, envisioning love stories as a daydreamer now fully awake.

Just Like Heaven

A love story of two individuals, each with their own identity and path, whose lives take an unexpected turn when tragedy strikes. In the midst of hardship, fate brings them together, forging a deep connection. As they navigate life's challenges side by side, their bond grows stronger, and love blossoms in the most unexpected moments.

A life she led on her own terms
Made her form and wit firm
The life she led was no cheer.
Because she was always competing with her peers.
The life she led had no fun.
As she was always on the run
Her morning started with people in bed lying
Her night ended with people in bed dying.
A sudden tragedy that hit her life
And had to find a way to survive
Her body and mind were lying dead.
But her soul was wondering, trying to find a shade.

Another soul suffered a dear one's loss
Holding this trauma, his head would toss
A life where he was heavily betrayed
The feeling of love was so strong now it felt so estranged.
The pain made him agonise.
That his brain could not analyse

One day he met this wandering soul.
They had both suffered and were in a big black hole.
He was the knight who could see her, hear her and bear her soul.
She was the one who could only be seen and heard by this
dynamic soul.

A magical connection has now formed.
Their hearts warmed up, their souls lit up.
Now they were back from their deep sleep.
Making their way forward on this big leap

They needed each other to define their roles.
They needed each other to heal their souls.

In Every Heartbeat

She lies awake through sleepless nights, longing for him, dreaming of his touch, yet finding only emptiness. She needs him, craves him, wishes endlessly to be by his side, where her heart truly belongs.

Those silent cries when I miss you
Those days I pray hard for strength as I feel you.
Those moments I ask for patience when waiting feels so hopeless.

Those tough days when I simply wait to hear your voice
Those nights when I long to see your face in my dreams.

Those times when my heart can't contain the need to touch you
Those moonlit nights when I manifest you to love me.
Those dark nights when I scream out your name, hoping you can hear me.

Those tired mornings when life feels worthless without you.
Those daunting dawns when you seem like a lost love.
Those aches in my heart when I try to let go of you.

Each day and night, learning to live without you.
Each day and night, trying to find answers to this soulful love.
Each day and night, praying for us to reconnect and start a new story.

Every moment seems painful with thoughts of you.
Every moment feels worthless without you by my side.

Every moment, I just can't help feeling this immense love for you.
Like my every heartbeat just breathes your name

Perfectly Flawed

She embraces her imperfections with grace, turning vulnerabilities into strengths that draw people in. Her authenticity shines through, making her both relatable and utterly unique.

You are, after all, just a human form, with feelings and attitude. You are good, and you are bad... You have your Yin and Yan moments. You are luminescent, but you can also be disastrous.

Because you are so Perfectly Flawed

You are very righteous, but you are also proud to be sinful. You are gracious, and sometimes inconsiderate.
You can emit light when needed, and at the same time, embrace the darkness within you.

After all, you are Perfectly Flawed.

You can be conventional, but your other side will also be progressive. You are vigorous, but you have a right to feel feeble, accept the weakness. After all, it's only YOU.
You don't always have to have a demeanor, you can show your vulnerable side, a need to be needed.

Thus, you are Perfectly Flawed

You are a tapestry woven with both brilliance and blunder.
An imperfection is not weaknesses, but the endearing edges of your compelling character.
You gained your quirks and scars, wearing them like badges of honor,
Self-acceptance makes you magnetic, a refreshing beacon of realness in a polished manner.

That is why you are Perfectly Flawed

Accept the war that is within you, and be proud to show off those scars. You don't have to rebuild yourself immediately, swim in the tears of sorrow, and rejuvenate yourself.
You are an equilibrium of radiance and dimness.

That is why you are Beautifully Flawed.

Reminiscing in Harmony

Years had passed, but as they sat together, laughter and nostalgia filled the air. They relieved their old love in fleeting glances and familiar smiles, not to rekindle, but to cherish what once was. As they parted, they wished each other happiness, knowing some love stories are meant to live in memories.

The evening was cold and cozy.
The air was fresh and breezy.

They were longing to see each other.
They were waiting to meet each other.

A sudden feeling of warmth was in the skies when they gazed
each other in the eyes.
Greetings of hi, hello and smiling faces made their spirit uprise.

Meeting after years and reminiscing about beautiful times
And a yearning to know how life has now been defined.

So many things to say, so many words to hear.
Sharing adventures, their smiles were full of cheer.

The life they had, the love they endured, lingered somewhere,
But this meetup made them respect their lost love and despair.

The past now feels like a beautiful story.
Walking down memory lane had its own glory.

The feeling of love has now changed into admiration,
The feeling of being together is now transformed into gratification.

The dive into each other's past made them acknowledge the love that had passed.
Narrating their sweet tales, beaming hearty smiles, the moonlight now lit the dark skies.

With no feeling of penitence and regret
They embraced each other, feeling joyful and blessed.

The Serene Landscape of Her Soul

Nature's embrace became her sanctuary and guide, Where she discovered a deep serenity inside. Her inner battles ceased, leaving her beautifully placid.

A journey into the unknown, yet the path felt deeply her own.
With open hands and fearless grace, she walked, time softening her pace.

Each leaf, each breeze, each dusky sky, a mirror held to what lived inside.
She welcomed all, storms and sun alike, each moment carving her spirit's light.

Each unfolding leaf, each sun-drenched stone, Mirrored the strength she had uniquely grown.
The very air, a mystic, freeing sigh, As nature's love enveloped her beneath the open sky.

Nature wrapped her in a sacred hush, a breath, a rhythm, a quiet rush.
Love poured in from the mountain and stream, the earth whispered truths she once called dream.
A freedom bloomed within her chest, a soft surrender, a longed-for rest.
In the hush of wind, she heard her name— no longer lost, no longer the same.

This hard-won calm, a wellspring deep inside, From which a vibrant inspiration did now ride.
The ancient wisdom whispered by the trees, Awakened an inner power, carried on the
gentle breeze.

The placid feeling, yearned for and so true, Now blossomed within, a long-awaited view.
The fierce internal battle, fought with grace, At last surrendered, finding solace in this sacred space.

In nature's tender hold, her truest self unfurled, A beautiful spirit, at peace with her own world.
The battle within, the ache, the plea, it dissolved in the stillness of every tree.
Now placid, whole, and undefined, she met her soul, and it was kind.

Release the Shackles

He is trapped in the weight of his own guilt, his emotions chaining him to a past he cannot escape. Unable to open up, he keeps his pain locked away—until she looks into his eyes and whispers, "Let it go. I have already forgiven you."

Why are you terrified of us?
Why are you fleeing from us?

You, avoiding me, display your guilt.
You, ignoring me, reflect your fear.

This heaviness you feel in your heart, whenever you recall our past
The shame you feel for your doings. Strive to bury them in ruins

When you think about us, your spirit explodes into dust.
What are you keeping hidden from yourself that you can't trust?

Be brave and confront me, and have the strength to admit it.
Accept your shortcomings and make peace with your past.

I know it enrages you to see, feel, and hear me.
But I have forgiven you...so set yourself free.

Let go of all your inhibitions
And embrace new beginnings.

Don't dwell on the past and suffer in the present.
I am no longer hurt because our experiences are no longer pertinent.

I pray that you overcome your feelings of grief and sorrow.
And set out on a new route to live a tranquil tomorrow.

Queen Of The Dark

She is the Queen of Dark, draped in power and radiating untouchable confidence. With unwavering strength, she seizes control, shaping destiny with her own hands. Fearless and flawless, she is the embodiment of perfection—unstoppable, unbreakable, and reigning in her own right.

She wore a crown of midnight on her head.
Her face shimmered when her wings spread.

In the radiant night, she charged her black hair strings.
On the night of the new moon, she fanned her fragrance in the air.

When she smiled, the trees stooped low.
With her touch the breeze would flow.

No fear could break her iron will,
No dawn could shake her kingdom still.

No sun dared to rise, and no fire dared to burn.
No stars dare to glow. No light wants to churn

Shadows clung in her realm, whispering secrets only she could hear.
She ruled not with words but in silence, the weapon she speared

She controlled the dusk and owned the land
The twilight in her presence would honour her stand

The demons would surrender to her essence.
The ancient lore would fear her very presence.

She was a monarch who was forever free, filled with dreams.
A storm, an empress and still an enigmatic being

She governed the shadows with a mystical mark.
She renounced herself as the 'Queen of the Dark'.

When Light Took Her Hand

In her darkest moments, she is burdened by grief and despair and finds unexpected solace in the presence of a calm, radiant soul—a divine guide or angelic figure. His quiet strength and unwavering light anchor her, helping her rediscover trust, hope, and the beauty of surrender. Through him, she learns to embrace life again, no longer afraid of the path ahead.

She had grown used to shadows, to walking beneath a sky that never broke, to silence louder than screams. Her days blurred, a slow ache beneath her skin, her soul wrapped in the cold hush of grief.

She wandered, not seeking direction, just distance—from the weight, from the haunted corners of her thoughts. Each step, a quiet surrender. Each breath, a prayer disguised as fatigue.

Then, like sunlight slipping through a crack, he appeared. Not with fanfare, but with the stillness of deep waters.
His presence, a hush in the storm. His voice, a balm, the wind carried gently to her wounds.

She didn't know what he was, a man? a guide? an angel shaped by stardust and time?
But his light did not blind her. It *met* her, softly, surely, like it had always known the way.

There was no command, no rescue cry, only an invitation. A gaze that saw past her ruin. Hands that steadied the trembling mast of her soul.

He anchored her, not by pulling her to shore, but by reminding her that even in the dark, she still floated. And she: weary of carrying the map alone, let go.

She trusted the compass he became. She leaned into the current he calmed. She never asked for proof. She didn't need a reason.

She simply surrendered: to the beauty, to the blessing, to the unfolding. Now, the road ahead does not terrify. The tunnel has a door. And she walks not behind him, but beside him, with light finally holding her hand.

Once a Flame, Now a Light

Their love was a quiet storm, fierce yet restrained. He was bound by vows, she by unspoken understanding. Though their hearts remained entwined forever, they accepted the distance fate had carved between them—loving in silence, honoring their separate worlds.

A lady of cheer and charm in her glow, a fellow who is reticent and striking in his flow.
In the quiet corners of a loud bar, an enchanting connection sparked the air.
In their joyful chatter, her heart was completely flattered.
In the laughter they shared, he found joy, and his heart flared.
Every whisper shared that night promised a warm sight.

Days turned to weeks, passions ignited, with each stolen embrace, their hearts delighted.
The union became so powerful, unaware of this bond seeming unlawful.

Their meeting was fated, though togetherness was waded
This tale of romance is so desirable, unfortunately filled with many obstacles.

They wore a smile, but it masked the ache, for love like theirs, they knew they had to break.
Their fondness was so gentle with the theme of tragic, but their hearts were filled with a dust of magic.
Though yearnings and distress, their love had no fortress.
Like their tale that was written, a love story which was forbidden

Seasons changed, time lapsed and life moved on, with love and acceptance.
Their souls are so pure, intertwined, welcoming a new relationship as life predefined.
What they meant, and what they'd be, their hearts still bound, yet roaming free.
No regrets, no mourning, as some bonds aren't lost, just softly embracing

A love born of passion, yet bound by the light, captured brightly, now etched in the night.
Now a deep and harmonious relationship, they named it a Soul companionship.

Misty Covert

She finds a thrill in secrets, treasuring the mystery they hold like hidden whispers only she understands. There's a certain magic in keeping them, a silent dance between truth and illusion that she alone controls. For her, the unknown is not frightening—it's intoxicating.

Secrets are meant to be concealed from this world.
Where your sins must be carefully preserved.

But her secrets are not always the misdeeds she wishes to hide.
Sometimes, they are a pleasure trip she loves to ride.

She hides her true self from the world.
Making sure Veracity of the story never fails.

People create different insight about her
And she delights in the aroma of this mysterious brew.

A thrilling puzzle she weaves within her being
Helps safeguard her well-being.

It's gratifying to be wrapped in a blanket.
And let her misdeeds and plans be forfeited.

Love's Lingering Ghost

Each morning, she tells herself it's over. Yet, in the quiet moments, his ghost still lingers, his touch warm in memory. No matter how far she moves forward, the past walks beside her, refusing to let go.

Though months have passed since their farewell sigh,
His memory still lingers in her whispering sky.
She longs for dawns where new hope gleams,
Yet love's soft shadows weave through her dreams.

Each time she extends her hand toward the new,
Determined to leave behind the ghosts of yesterday,
A once-warm heart now hails a chill of solitude,
Ensnared by spells that echo in lonely dismay

Each time a kiss she shares with a new one, it's a haunting trace
Her memory, very vivid, comes with a cruel embrace
Her mind becomes a battlefield of yesterday, as a feeling of guilt holds an unending sway

Her heart, a fortress, guarded and concealed, Afraid to trust, afraid to be healed

A past transgression, etched in deep, A wound she guards, a vow to keep
She builds her walls of ice and stone, Afraid to let her heart be known
For every touch, a chilling fear, That love's embrace will disappear
Anchored fast to yesterday's despair, she questions if she'll break the snare

Uncertain how much longer she can fight, Against the shadows of her endless night
Will dawn arrive to melt the frost, or will her spirit be forever lost?
Trapped within this haunting rhyme, A prisoner of space and time.

The path ahead, a shadowed maze, where moving on feels like a daze
Confined within these walls of pain, A prisoner of memory's chain
The bin of time, a distant shore, Where yesterday exists no more

The Star She Never Touched

She discovers a deep, soulful love she never expected—one born of signs, dreams, and silent knowing. Though she cannot hold it, she feels it fully, and with grace, she releases it, choosing peace over possession.

She had worn armor made of fire, marched through storms without a tremble on her desire. She thought herself forged in flame, fearless, unshaken, strong by name.
But one quiet day, a feather landed in her hands soft, unexpected, sent by stars she'd forgotten she once wished upon.

In the moonlight through the dark, came a soul who left a quiet mark.

The skies spoke in symbols: a flicker in dreams, a hush in the wind, a shadow that felt like sunlight.
Signs were whispered in silent skies, dreams bathed in cosmic replies. The universe, in sacred play, brought forth the prayer she used to say.

She had called for love in silence— and the universe had answered in a language only her soul could hear.

She did not know that her longing had been cradled, by something vast and unseen, that the chaos she danced in had always been a path carved with care.
A Love, long hidden, took its place, unfolding in gentleness with a mystic grace.

She never knew her ache was heard, nor that her chaos had been stirred, and shaped—by hands unseen but wise, delivering truth in soft disguise.
She didn't know the wish had landed, that destiny had gently handed, a mirror to the love she yearned, a fire for which her soul had burned.

The weight had settled, a cloak she'd long worn, Threads of expectation, tightly, fiercely sworn. She stood at the precipice, a whisper on the breeze, The echoes of old battles rustling through the trees.

Though she never saw her face, nor felt her touch, nor shared a place, but she felt the pulse, she loved her deep the moon adores the tide— from afar, yet entirely with a silent song she couldn't defend.

And then, the letting go, a sigh the earth might share, A loosening of grip, a breath of purest air. The phantom faded, its edges growing dim, No longer the conductor of her heart's soft hymn.

But the harder letting go, a tremor in her soul, The unraveling of "her," beyond her own control. She watched the pieces fall, not with a cry of pain, But with a quiet wonder, like a cleansing summer rain.

The Silent Storm

Depression feels like a heavy fog that dulls everything—thoughts, emotions, even the things you once loved. It's a quiet struggle, where even small tasks can feel overwhelming, and you're constantly fighting a sense of emptiness or hopelessness.

Her morning light awakens a longing within,
A yearning that gnaws, but her heart cannot win.

She wants to be set free from these feelings that cling like a body possessed by a devil
To let them vanish, and let peace take wing, she asks for her spirit to be settled

But the thought lingers, like a shadow that haunts the night,
The air is so deep and bleak, a weight that presses so tight.

Hearty and scary, a presence that always stays,
A constant reminder of heartache's beats sway.

Alone she sits, in an empty, hollow space,
Aimless and lost, with nothing to embrace.

A heaviness that holds a cry that cannot break,
A heart and mind entwined in an unfinished ache.

No escape, no refuge, no place to hide,
Trapped in this turmoil, where emotions reside.

Sleepless nights, filled with nightmares and fear,
Praying, crying, hoping that dawn will bring clarity here.

But alas, the sun sets once more,
Night creeps in, and the cycle begins anew, as before.

Morning arrives, and she wakes, still famished and worn,
Wishing these feelings would vanish, and peace be reborn.

The Possession

She felt the shadows crawl beneath her skin, A voice not hers whispering through her lips. By the time she realised, she was all engulfed in him.

A fierce night, an overwhelming sight
Amidst the darkness, so much sadness

Attracting an entity so powerful, gazing at her so lustful
Deep diving in her mind, It knew her heart was not assigned.

An easy target, an easy catch. He played along to make a match.
Making her sleep, it crowded her mind very deep

She saw this blur figure in her dream, and made her go under its sweam
The hint of curiosity could not hold her back, but she got caught up in its mien, so dark.

It invaded her in the purest form. Now she was engulfed in this swarm.
It bonded her mind and heart, compelling her to act its part.

She felt so trapped in its allure, it was nothing but a venomous hunter.
The hunger was so eloquent, its disposition so dominant.

She tried to fight this demonic entity, but succumbed to its supremacy.
She struggled with its delirium, feeling inept by this cynicism.

Making her fragile and weak...Alas, she gave into its transgression.
Nowhere to escape, nowhere to elude, she just surrendered to this possession.

The Blurred Lines of Love

A trace of her emotional journey through the ambiguities of love, exploring the uncertainties of their connection. It examines the shift in her feelings when she perceives neglect, regardless of intent, and how her love persists through anger and frustration, questioning....what is this?

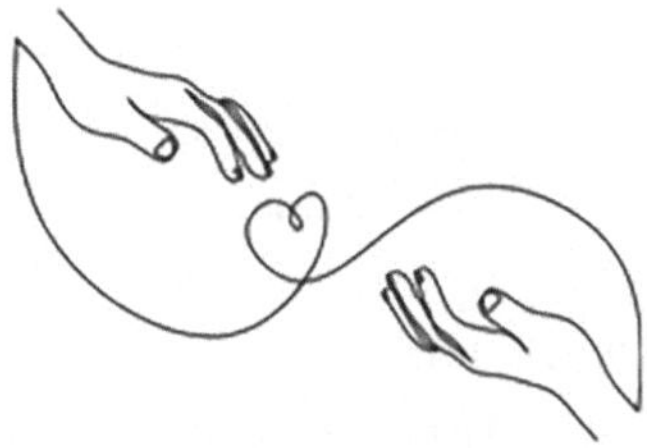

His presence instantly transforms her mood, filling her with joy radiating from her countenance.
Her face lights up like a sunrise, reflecting the inner warmth and happiness he ignites within her soul.

Yet, in stark contrast, his absence leaves her feeling utterly empty and desolate,
Her emotional world crumbled, leaving behind a void where vibrant feelings once celebrate.

An emotional rollercoaster, feeling disoriented, powerless, and vulnerable
The passion she seeks, the care she seeks, makes her insufferable

As a sense of hope filled her, illuminating a path she had not seen, leaving her wondering, "Is this love?"

A constant need for his presence and the fear of its eventual absence
A persistent undercurrent of longing tugs at her heart, unable to control his essence

Her thoughts of him, they speak, as day succumbs to night's glow.
In slumber's hush, his image stays, A constant guest, in her mind he flows

In dreams, his presence is felt so true, A shadow that dances, with thoughts anew
Upon waking, the dawn's early light, she finds his memory still, a lingering as dew

These complex emotions continue to baffle her, She finds herself pondering, "Is this really love?"

As he showers her with care and attention, her love for him blossoms and flourishes
Like a vibrant flower basking in the sunlight of his affection

But when he, in haste, does stray, her heart, once full of love, now feels dismayed
A wave of resentment, swift and cold, washes over her, and she feels played

To be seen, to be heard, to be known, is all she seeks, in love's tender throne.
But in his neglect, though unintended, She feels a sting, and her heart moan.

Again, she traversed the complex terrain of her emotions, reflecting on the transformations. The question echoed within her: 'Is this what love does to you?'"

He draws a smile from her lips and fills her with a sense of delight
A feeling she cherishes and craves, and her heart shines bright

Her heart soars with elation when he speaks, hanging onto every word he says
Every inflection in his voice, she ceased, leaving her yearning for more of those days

His touch transformed every aspect of her life, a deep affection and passion she had suppressed
Newfound feelings, fresh and invigorating, reviving her spirit like her soul being caressed

Filling her with a sense of hope she hadn't felt before. With a hopeful heart, she couldn't help but ask herself, "Is this true love"?

Uncertain of her feelings, she questions her unwavering thoughts
She yearns for an eternity with him, but doubts creep in, whispering naught

In the depth of her adoration for him, whispers of angst of this ardent passion
She searches for answers, night and day, to the question that haunts her, conviction

She holds onto a hope in her heart, A glimmer of faith, that they will never be apart.
For in the darkness, a whisper she does hear, A gentle reminder, that love can persevere.

Torn between the intensity of her emotions, she struggles to discern, "Is she obsessed, or is this love?"

The Night Of No Mercy

He played with her heart like it was a game, Not knowing she'd turn the ending herself

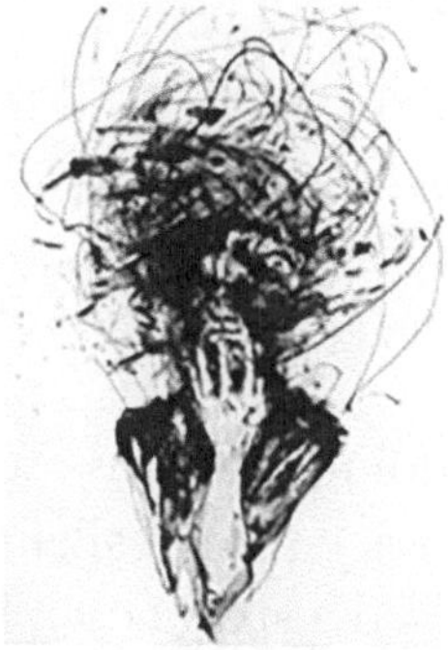

A dark and dreadful night, rain showering, no one in sight
With a cynical smile, a dead body next to her lie
Her hands painted crimson red, his heart torn into shreds.
The power of malevolence is a betrayal in the face of endlessness.

A story of love at first sight, a perfect romantic tale.
He was smart, handsome, and she was beautiful and frail.
In stolen breaths, tender touch the affection so deep
The world dissolved, and now time ceased to be

A spark ignited which was wild and raw. She was completely in awe.
He swept her off her feet, and she danced along his beat.
She was love-struck, a boundless thrill.
When she was with him, the world grew still

Her desire for him became intense. Unaware it was all a pretense!!

His smile was a mask and his heart was untrue.
Under all the flattery words, a dark shadow brews.
His heart was treacherous, a tale he'd hide
He was already married to a beautiful bride.

The veil could not hide; these deceitful eyes, this love game of passion, turned into a crime of violence.

A trust was shattered, bruised, and torn, in secret halls where lies convene
An unwavering whisper in her ear, "I seek revenge for wove betrayal so cold and mean."
Her form was unemotional, and the wounds burned inside.
A fierce in her lens and body full of vengeful pride.

She questioned his doings and love: why was it betrayed?
No answer to his misdeed; he stood silently, ashamed and afraid.
Her heart pulsed a spark, each breath a pyre.

Her fists clenched tight, her veins ran red with wrath's own fire.
She pierced the silver dagger to end his throbbing heartbeat.
An end to this misery, as she saw him plaintively bleat.
An act so brutal, she showed no remorse, just her thoughts now slowly dispersed.
A peaceful air of presence, a content in her essence.

The Love She Thought She'd Never Find

Story of a woman who, after facing heartbreak and self-doubt from shallow connections, begins to question her worth. Just as she loses hope, she meets someone who sees and loves her fully, helping her rediscover herself and what true love really means.

Who is she meant to be, she sighed, A giver of joy while her own dreams died?
A muse for fleeting, selfish fires, A caregiver bound by others' desires?

She wandered hearts like empty halls, Met men who built her just to fall.
They spoke in promises, soft and sweet, But vanished like rain in desert heat.

They spoke of admiration, of beauty they could see,
But none had touched the core, the wild and yearning "she."

Each name she whispered into night Left shadows, everlasting light.
She searched for love in hollow eyes, Yet found reflections dressed in lies.

With time, the mirror turned her foe, *"Am I too much or not enough?"* she'd grow.
She questioned every scar and part, And bore the weight of a breaking heart.

And in the lonely hours, beneath the moon's pale gleam,
A bitter self-reproach would steal into her dream.

She saw her flaws magnified, her worth diminished low,
A silent, inner battle where self-hatred seemed to grow.

Then, through the tangled pathways, where her weary spirit trod,
A presence unexpected, a gift sent by a god,
One day, beneath a twilight sky, A gentle soul came drifting by.

No armor worn, no boastful claim, No need to win, no hunger for fame.
He saw her—not the mask or role, But every fracture, every whole.

He looked beyond the surface, the smiles she'd learned to wear,
And saw the fragile beauty, the burdens that she'd bear.

He held her hand like sacred art, And kissed the ruins of her heart.
He listened to her silences, too, And showed her what real love can do.

Not built on want, or need, or game, But knowing someone and loving them the same.
Through him, she met herself anew, The child, the storm, the sky so blue.

And in his loving mirror, her own reflection changed,
The self-loathing diminished, the bitterness estranged.

No prince in tales, just man and muse,
But finally, love she didn't have to lose.

And in his arms, she finally understood the art,
The selfless, deep connection that sets two souls apart.

He showed her what it meant, to be truly seen and known,
And in that radiant knowing, she was finally her own.

The "who she's meant to be" no longer felt obscure,
But a woman deeply cherished, in a love that would endure.

Silenced Cries, Unspoken Truths

A story which again went unheard of so many rape victims- A wound dismissed, a voice unheard. Now, they are just another forgotten name in a story no one wants to read

A dreadful story which was untold
She kept it away for so long, today to unfold

A tremble in her voice, sobbing and choking as she spoke
Her body full of fear, her heart pumped to a stroke.

He came onto me like a wildfire, seizing my bod.
This sudden ambush made me numb to the core.
I struggled to set myself loose,
But his strength was a heavy noose.
I cried, I begged for myself to be free.
But his hunger overpowered my screams.
Bound by chains unseen, he kept thrusting his needs.
I laid there captive, shunning my pleads.

My eyes teared, sensing my drained fame.
And my shadow burned, like a flickering flame.
Through tangled thorns and this fearful night,
I sought the dawn, to a promised light
The morning awakened, my essence still shivered.

My form was conquered but my soul not yet, delivered"
And she asked aloud….
"For just a taste of lustful content, what joy could rise from such a blight?
To crush her shining wings, to dim her soul, and steal its light"

A narrative told by many, now the world also does not find these plights uncanny.
She became just another chronicle, and her tale, one day, will be historical.

Rooted in Trust

Through every joy and storm, their bond remained unshaken—love deeper than words. They promised to stand by each other, not as lovers, but as lifelong companions, knowing some souls are meant to walk together forever.

Their bond was intellectual and in high regards
This is how they'd describe their friendship with guards.

A soulful tie that nature had planned
Each other's emotions they'd understand

Their relationship was questioned by many.
They would enjoy the misconception and would find it quite funny.

Through laughter's peaks and sorrow's shade,
A profound connection was deeply made.

No jealousy felt, no possessive chains
Just honest care without any selfish gains

They stood for each other through thick and thin.
Always wished and prayed for each other within

An innate relationship with close emotional ties
A bond of strength, just honest trust in caring eyes.

In storms of life, when anchors failed
A hearty conversation just made the day.

A friendship untouched by time and place
Rooted in trust with a soul connection that stays

Where in this world where few remain,
Their friendship stood—both pure and plain.

Shadows of Desire

For one night, they were lost in each other—whispers, warmth, and a fleeting kind of magic. No promises, no regrets, just the perfect collision of two souls. And sometimes, in the quiet of the night, she still feels the ghost of his touch.

She walked by the shore listening to the waves roar.
Her thoughts playing a song, her heart thumping like a gong
This beautiful twilight reminded her of a sensuous night.

An enchanting saga, a secret she hides beneath her soul
An alluring experience. In her mind it always scrolls.

No promises they made, no ties bind, just fun fleeting moments, got intertwined.
The touch sparked a fire. Every kiss made their bodies desire
No words were needed, only huffing breath, as they surrendered to their essence depth.

A passion so fierce, but the rhythm pure. In each embrace, they did feel secure.
Their bodies united, hearts beating fast. All the thoughts now become their past.
Every move, soft and strong, was like music playing an endless song.

As the night faded to dawn, this intimacy in memory was drawn.
No chains to hold, no need to stay. Just one last embrace, and they slipped away.
In this exciting adventure, they found a worldly release, an encounter so profound, they were in perfect peace.

Strolling through the echoes of that day always makes her heart sway.
With a yearning smile and a hope so slight, she dreams of reliving that amazing night.

To Love, To Live, To Feel

"To live unchained, to love without walls, And to feel every ache and joy deeply — That is the art of being alive."

We are designed to fall in love.
We are equipped to feel all emotions.

Our bodies are made to desire connections.
Our hearts always give us directions.

And yet we resist, what we observe, what we need.
We stop ourselves from feeling too deep.

We fear hurt, resentment and losing people.
We fear attachment, emptiness and our minds battle

So we try to maintain an illusion of control, trying to be strong
and calm the waters down.
And we forget to flow, we forget to let the feeling, feel completely
Because we know this will end someday, innately.
And yes, it will hurt, and we will feel worse.

But then that's life!

Nothing is permanent, not even our forms.
So break all the barriers, just live for now, and experience the Magic.
The way nature is designed to allow flowers to bloom.
It's better to feel something than not to feel anything.

True Reflections

"She walked through the ruins of what broke her, And in the quiet, she met the woman she was meant to be. Peace wasn't given — she found it within."

Amidst this beautiful creation, she found her true reflections.

She is here to find her place, to heal, to feel the love she's embraced.
This wonderful life she has ventured, and was thrilled with all her adventures.

All the chaos in her rind, but always a path she would find.
The craziness in her always made her flur
The joy in her always made her live life a little more.

Every flaw in her, she made a beautiful narrative.
The world to dig deep and see her life, so creative.

She knew she was enough, a form of divinity above
A perfectly created masterpiece, filled with true love

With every scar and every pain, she created a perfect song.
A pleasing euphony in a poetic form that made her stand strong.

In her truest form of light she will always shine bright.
In the world's unsteady dream, she will create a perfect sight.

Amidst this beautiful creation, she found her true reflections.

Veil of Deception

He spins sweet lies, thinking she's falling for every word. But she's watching closely, fully aware of the game he's playing — letting him dig his own grave.

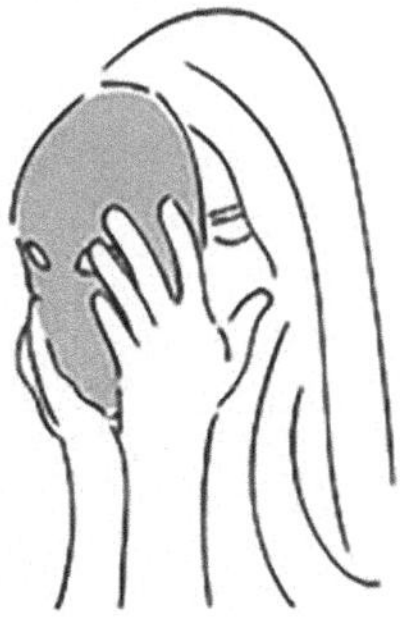

You deceive me every time we meet.
You make up stories every time we speak.

Please don't assume I'm naive; I know you lie.
As though I'm unaware of how many times you've flipped

I see through you, through your guiltful eyes.
I watch your actions when your words fall dry.

I soulfully play around, assuming I am being fooled.
You throw loving words, but all your actions are discerned.

Your air is gray where clarity falters and doubt takes root.
And I wear a mask and pretend like I enjoyed the fruit.

The falsehood cannot be hidden and buried forever.
The deepest shadows also see light when uncovered.

You are lying to me, and I am tricking you.
Enjoying this pretense, seeing I win or you.

Whispers of the Last Drink

Intoxication crept into his life like a sweet escape, but quietly stole everything he held dear. What began as a refuge soon became a chain, pulling him away from love, purpose, and peace.

He was a man of great demeanor and a soul filled with love.
An affectionate person so generous, people adored him for his boldness.
Family loved him for his solemness, a thriving lad, but full of calmness.

But one day his story turned into a devil's own tale.
Betrayed in love, lost in life, his narration is quite a deep dive.
Questioning his fate, asking for an answer being innate

He dwelled in this sorrow, he lingered long, his body wrapped in a haunting song.
With remorse and regret in his core, he could not find solace in his bode.
He wandered far from light and grace, nothingness he had embraced.

Meandering around, in the twilight hours, someone called a bottle. A spell empowers
With each pour his worries drowned, with each thought more glass downed.
In every sip, a fleeting thrill, a broken piece he would instill

Days blurred, nothing but a haze, people fading in his drunken maze.
Still drinking in silence, trying to numb the pain, each step takes him closer to abstain
A blank stare, a heavy breath, he tasted the kiss of waiting death.
No dawn to break, nothing to embed, just empty bottles, now whispers dead

Wings Unbound

Her spiritual awakening and subsequent understanding of the world led to a profound transformation of her thoughts.

The soul seems free now, floating above the clouds.
Feeling vivacious and unconfined, she raised her spirits high.
Cheers to the universe for all the good she deserves.
Gratitude towards her Angels for all the knowledge she preserves
She stood tall under the golden sun.
Feeling pleased for all that she has won

The sight of being liberated from worldly affairs
A celestial energy breathing in the air
This transformation keeps her curious.
Realizing that the life she lived is so factitious
A journey she thought she pursued
It was very unlike the spiritual walk which blossomed.

Sensation of awakening to the essence of her being
The feeling of emancipation made her body transform.
Climbing the heavenly stairs with elegance
Shining herself in excellence
This spiritual journey she has acclaimed
A journey so beautiful seems unexplained

Life is a Miracle

Life is a miracle, a beautiful journey unfolding in its own time. Embrace it with love, let go of worries, and trust the flow. When you surrender to the rhythm of life, everything falls into place just as it should.

Life is a miracle. A lovely puzzle
Just be acceptable, and believe in this wonderful existence.

Understand life is never consistent
As both good and terrible, they will eventually disappear.
Savour each moment as it arises.
As life just happens to us

Life is a miracle. A lovely puzzle
Just be acceptable, and believe in this wonderful existence.

People come and go
Embrace everything that you sow
Memories are created
As everything is related

Life is a miracle. A lovely puzzle
Just be acceptable, and believe in this wonderful existence.

Your presence itself is so beautiful.
Our amalgamation with the creator is graceful.
Believe and Trust Life is just a mystery.
Every new day creates a magnificent story.